DRAGONS around the World

A Field Guide

TAYLOR FENMORE

Lerner Publications ◆ Minneapolis

Content consultant: Juwen Zhang

Lerner Publications Company
An imprint of Lerner Publishing Group, Inc.
241 First Avenue North
Minneapolis, MN 55401 USA

For reading levels and more information, look up this title at www.lernerbooks.com.

Main body text set in Aptifer Sans LT Pro.
Typeface provided by Linotype AG.

Editor: Angel Kidd **Designer:** Athena Currier **Photo Editor:** Lucien Brinkley

Library of Congress Cataloging-in-Publication Data

Names: Fenmore, Taylor, author.
Title: Dragons around the world : a field guide / Taylor Fenmore.
Description: Minneapolis, MN : Lerner Publications, [2026] | Series: Dragon field guides | Includes bibliographical references and index. | Audience: Ages 8–11 | Audience: Grades 4–6 | Summary: "Myths about dragons span centuries and continents. Readers will travel the globe and learn the similarities and differences between many fascinating types of dragons, such as European wyrms, Chinese long, Australian rainbow serpents, and more"— Provided by publisher.
Identifiers: LCCN 2024041660 (print) | LCCN 2024041661 (ebook) | ISBN 9798765669310 (library binding) | ISBN 9798765683996 (paperback) | ISBN 9798765676974 (epub)
Subjects: LCSH: Dragons—Juvenile literature. | Dragons—Folklore—Juvenile literature. | Animals, Mythical—Juvenile literature.
Classification: LCC GR830.D7 F46 2026 (print) | LCC GR830.D7 (ebook) | DDC 398.24/54—dc23/eng/20240909

LC record available at https://lccn.loc.gov/2024041660
LC ebook record available at https://lccn.loc.gov/2024041661

Manufactured in the United States of America
1-1011747-53902-1/3/2025

Table of Contents

A Storm on the Lake

Mishipeshu swims slowly through the water. Legend has it this wingless dragon lives in Lake Superior. It moves through watery tunnels deep beneath the lake's surface.

Then it stops. When it speaks, its hissing voice sounds like rushing water. It starts to create waves. Then the water swirls into a whirlpool. Soon Mishipeshu causes a storm on the lake. People riding in boats must be careful on the rough waters.

Mishipeshu is one of many dragons that appear in stories from North American cultures. But people from all around the world have told stories about dragons throughout history. African and Australian dragons are often connected to nature.

This ancient rock painting shows Mishipeshu, a water spirit from Ojibwe myths.

Asian dragons are said to bring good fortune. European dragons are linked to evil and greed.

People tell stories about dragons for many reasons. A dragon is often a symbol of an idea, feeling, or event. This means that there are many different dragon stories—and many different kinds of dragons! What other dragons exist in cultures around the world? And what do people think of them?

CHAPTER 1
Dragons of Asia

Dragons are important in many Asian cultures. Most of these dragons are snakelike with long bodies, four claws, and crests around their heads. Many are connected to nature and power. Even if they don't have wings, they can usually fly.

The Long

Dragons are called long, lung, or loong in China and Vietnam. Chinese long have four or five claws. They control the wind and bring rain for crops. Long are connected to power, wealth, and luck.

A traditional Chinese dragon dance being performed for the Lunar New Year in Liverpool, England, in 2023

Since at least the third century BCE, people have made puppets that look like dragons to dance with during special rituals. These rituals began as a way to honor ancestors and bring good fortune. People still do them for fun and to celebrate the Lunar New Year.

Like the Chinese long, the Vietnamese long are lucky. They bring rainfall for crops. These long are connected to water in other ways too. Many waterways in Vietnam, such as the Ha Long Bay and the Cuu Long, are named after them. *Ha Long* means "descending dragon." *Cuu Long* means "River of Nine Dragons."

A dragon statue overlooks West Lake in Hanoi, Vietnam.

Many European dragons in stories breathed fire to scare or hurt people.

FACT VS. FICTION

All dragons are good.

FICTION!

Dragons from Asia are often seen as good. They help people. Some can even tell the future. But dragons from other cultures might be seen as bad or symbols of bad things. That's because people often told stories about dragons to understand the world. Dragons in stories could be helpful by bringing rain in a drought. Or they could be symbols of bad or evil things such as greed. But if dragons were real, they probably wouldn't be all good or all bad.

A dragon statue on a South Korean temple

The Yong and the Ryu

Korean dragons are called yong. Like the long, they are wingless and snakelike. They also have four claws and may have crests. But they are said to have other animal traits too, such as rabbit eyes.

In myths, the yong are patient and noble. They are also symbols of wisdom, power, and good fortune. Kings put designs of these dragons on their robes to show that they were powerful but fair. Many Korean buildings, especially temples for worship, have dragon statues.

The ryu or tatsu are from Japan. Unlike long, the ryu only have three claws. But they are still signs of power, wealth, and luck. Some myths say that Japan's first ruler descended from dragons.

DRAGON DRUMS

Korean people have painted dragons on barrel drums throughout history. These dragon drums are traditionally used in folk or court music.

A nine-headed dragon statue at a shrine in Japan

Statues of ryu are often near temples or shrines. They are symbols of good fortune. Some people say they protect the gods who are worshipped there.

Bakunawa

Bakunawa is a sea dragon from the Philippines. It has gills and two sets of wings. It lives deep within the ocean. This dragon was once said to cause lunar eclipses.

Ancient Filipinos may have considered the Bakunawa a connection between their world and the cosmos. Modern people still show the Bakunawa in art, music, and stories. It reminds them to respect nature and the cosmos.

CHAPTER 2

Dragons of Europe

Unlike Asian dragons, European dragons are usually seen as bad or even dangerous. Most breathe fire. Some attack people. They are often symbols of human traits such as evil or greed.

Ancient Greek and Roman Dragons

Countless dragon myths come from ancient Rome and Greece. These dragons are often described as powerful and even deadly. Some have powers that people compared to those of the gods. People often saw all these dragons as bad.

An illustration of a chimera from 1792

In Greece, such dragons were often split into four groups. The dracaenae have the upper body of a woman and the lower body of a dragon. Dracones are giant serpents, sometimes with more than one head. The cetea are sea monsters. Chimeras are a mix of a lion, a snake, and a goat.

Wyrms

Wyrms come from northern Europe. They are large serpents. Some have wings and others don't. Some have crests around their head.

Many wyrms do not fly or breathe fire. But some can poison people and animals with their breath or bite. Many people thought killing a wyrm was heroic. Wyrms and other dragons represented sin in some European religions, so killing them meant removing an evil from the world.

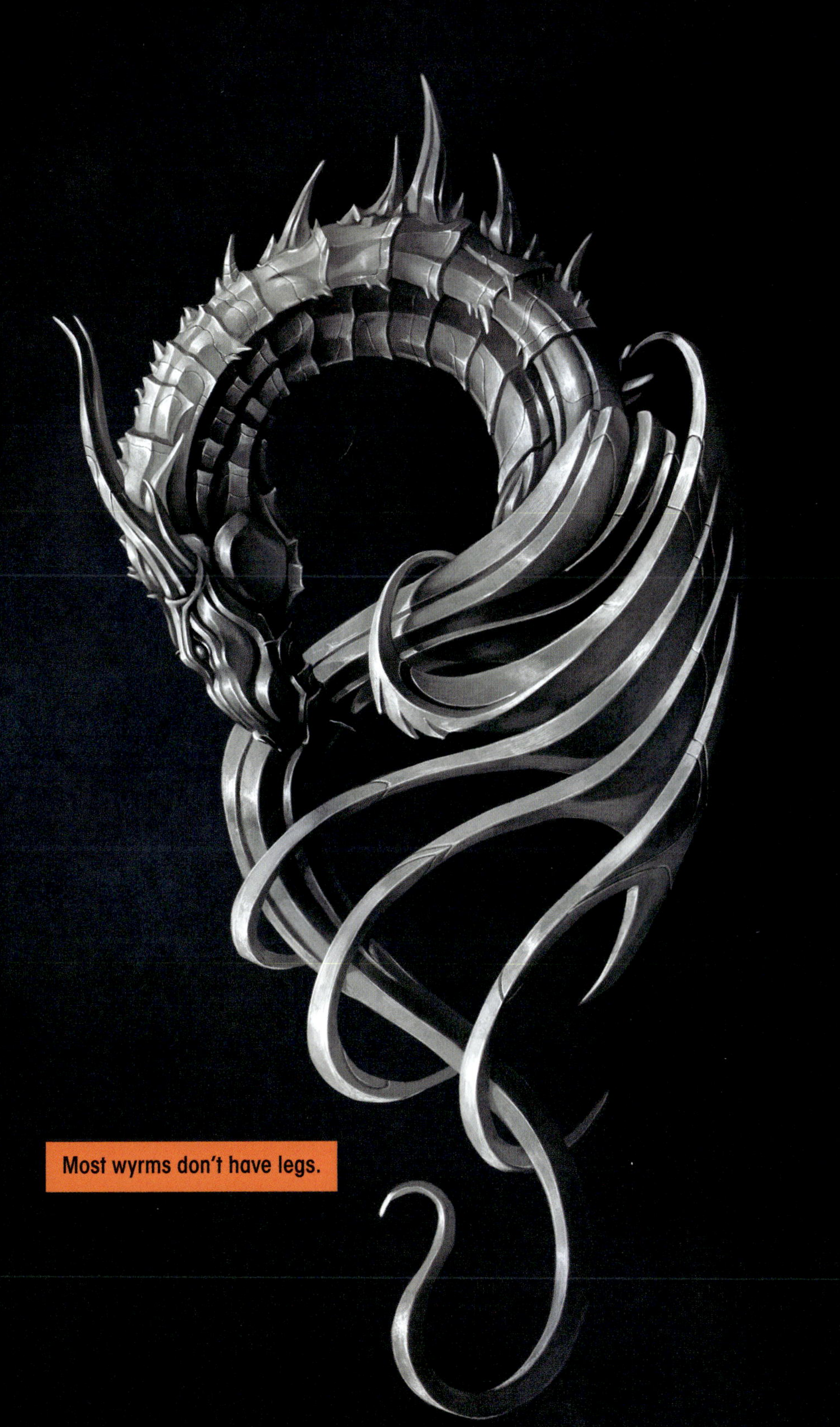

Most wyrms don't have legs.

Fafnir protected his treasure from many before he was slain.

A Tale from Norse Myths

Fafnir was a dwarf from Norse stories who killed his father to take his gold. His greed turned him into a dragon. He had sharp claws, wings, and tough scales. He breathed fire and spent a lot of time guarding treasure. A hero slayed him.

Fafnir is a symbol of greed. People told his story to warn against wanting too much wealth or power. But they also told it to show that greed could be stopped.

LEGEND OF THE TATZELWURM

Tatzelwurms have no wings. They are a dragon that is a mix of a cat and a snake. They hunt animals and sometimes humans.

Tatzelwurm legends began in the Alpine region of Europe.

CHAPTER 3
Dragons of the Americas and Australia

Some dragons from American and Australian cultures are believed to cause trouble. Others have important ties to nature and the cosmos.

The Piasa Bird

The story of the Piasa bird comes from the Illiniwek in North America. This dragon has wings, clawed feet, horns, and a long tail. Scales cover its body.

Piasa means "bird that devours people." People see it as a monster. It swoops down from cliffs to attack and eat people. Few images of it exist. One is a painting on a cliff in Illinois, but it is not the original. Some people think an Illiniwek group first created the painting and fired arrows at it to show their bravery. The arrows ruined the original, so modern artists re-created it.

The re-created cliff painting of the Piasa bird in Illinois

Quetzacóatl and the Amaru

Many South American dragons are connected to nature or the underworld. Quetzacóatl is a god that takes on the shape of a flying, feathered dragon or snake. He symbolizes many ideas, including art and knowledge. Some say he invented the calendar and books. He is also the god of wind.

Quetzacóatl is connected to ideas about life and death too. Many groups, including the Maya, Aztecs, Toltecs, and Olmec, worshipped him. Some people still do.

MANY FORMS

Quetzacóatl is often shown as a dragon. But he is said to take other forms too. One form is a bearded man.

Quetzacóatl is sometimes shown with wings and sometimes without.

The Amaru comes from Inca myths. It is often two-headed and snakelike. Sometimes it has wings or is shown as a few different animals mixed together.

The Amaru lives underground. This dragon is said to cause earthquakes when it moves and to affect the shape of the earth. Stories about the Amaru helped explain how the world was made. Amaru is still a symbol in many artworks and festivals of Indigenous groups in the Andes region.

Incas may have worshipped creatures such as Amaru at Machu Picchu.

An Aboriginal mural of a Rainbow Serpent

Australian Rainbow Serpent

The Rainbow Serpent Eingana appears in Aboriginal Australian myths. It is often shown as snakelike and colorful. People told stories about the Rainbow Serpent to help explain natural events and how life began. They believed this dragon caused rainbows when it moved from one waterhole to another. Eingana was also thought to have created the world.

CHAPTER 4
Dragons of Africa

Many dragons of African culture have ties to nature and life. Some cause safe natural events such as rainbows. Others warn of danger.

Bida

The legend of Bida comes from Ghana and Mali. Bida is a huge dragon and sometimes considered a great serpent. Some people say it has black scales, bat wings, and four claws.

Human sacrifices were given to Bida so that it would bring rain and gold to the people. Bida can also make itself invisible. Because of this, it is a symbol of dread.

Ninki Nanka of the Gambia

Ninki Nanka comes from West Africa, especially the Gambia. It is sometimes shown as a snakelike creature with black-and-green scales, three horns, and a feathered crest.

Ninki Nanka usually served as a warning. People believed that if you saw it, you would grow ill or die. People also told their children about Ninki Nanka so the children wouldn't go near swamps. They said the dragon would come out and steal them.

Ninki Nanka served as a warning against going to places such as this mangrove forest in the Gambia.

African Rainbow Serpent

Tales of the Rainbow Serpent Aido-Hwedo came out of Dahomey in West Africa. As they did with Bida, people sometimes called him a great serpent.

Aido-Hwedo was a powerful symbol of nature. Some people considered him a god. People believed he helped create the world. He was also thought to cause natural events such as rainbows and earthquakes.

Aido-Hwedo is often depicted eating his tail.

HUNGRY FOR IRON

Aido-Hwedo eats the metal iron to stay strong! If there isn't enough iron, he might also eat his own tail. People say that if he finishes his tail, the world will end.

Worldwide Dragons

Dragons are symbols of many things, from good luck to evil. In ancient stories, they helped explain how rain falls, what causes earthquakes, and how the world began. People often gave gifts to dragons so that they could receive their help or be assured the dragons would not hurt them.

Dragon stories have come out of every part of the world. They can mean different things to different people. After hearing some of these stories, what do you think of these dragons? What are other dragons you've heard of? Talk about it with a friend. Maybe you'll learn more about the wyrms of Europe or yong of Korea. Or maybe you'll come up with a whole new list!

A Look at Rainbow Serpents

The naga of Thailand are sometimes shown as Rainbow Serpents.

Rainbow Serpents appear in many cultures around the world. Most live in bodies of water such as rivers or lakes. Some even carve new rivers when they move through the mud. These snakelike dragons often have no legs. Only some have wings. But they can all fly. They are named for their colors. Some Rainbow Serpents are sky blue. Some are striped red and yellow. And others are many different colors.

Glossary

Aboriginal: of or relating to the Indigenous peoples of Australia

cosmos: the universe, especially when in balance, order, or harmony

crest: a showy growth of skin, fur, or feathers on or around the head of an animal

descend: to be related by blood through many generations

Illiniwek: a group of about a dozen Indigenous nations from the Mississippi River Valley in North America

lunar eclipse: an event in which Earth's shadow hides the moon

myth: a story often with imaginative creatures, people, and events that explain history, beliefs, or something else

Norse: of or relating to ancient Scandinavia

ritual: a ceremonial act or action

sin: actions against religious law or rules

symbolize: to represent or stand for something

underworld: the place of the souls of the dead in some cultures

Learn More

Britannica Kids: Quetzalcóatl
https://kids.britannica.com/kids/article/Quetzalc%C3%B3atl/476724

Kaiser, Brianna. *Dragon Folklore: A Field Guide*. Minneapolis: Lerner Publications, 2026.

Kiddle: Bakunawa Facts for Kids
https://kids.kiddle.co/Bakunawa

Kiddle: Chinese Dragon Facts for Kids
https://kids.kiddle.co/Chinese_dragon

Orsi, Tea. *The Great Book of Dragon Legends*. New York: White Star Kids, 2023.

Rea, Amy C. *Dragons of Norse Mythology*. Minneapolis: Kids Core, 2024.

Index

Photo Acknowledgments

Image credits: benedek/Getty Images, p. 5; wellsie82/Getty Images, p. 7; Kat Clay/Getty Images, p. 8; Coneyl Jay/Getty Images, p. 9; BobGrif/Getty Images, p. 10; Richard Sharrocks/Getty Images, p. 11; dokosola/Shutterstock, p. 12; Olaf Kruger/Getty Images, p. 14; Keynari/Shutterstock, p. 15; Arthur Rackham (Public Domain), p. 16; BlueLotusArt/Shutterstock, p. 17; Wirestock, Inc./Alamy, p. 19; calavera roja/Shutterstock, p. 21; Kelly Cheng/Getty Images, p. 22; Bill Bachman/Alamy, p. 23; mariusz_prusaczyk/Getty Images, p. 25; Danita Delimont/Alamy, p. 26; Nan_Got/Shutterstock, p. 28. Design elements: NikonLamp/Shutterstock; Lukasz Szwaj/Shutterstock; vi73/Shutterstockl; T Studio/Shutterstock; VartB/Shutterstock.

Cover: Arthur Balitskii/Shutterstock.